MW00328250

GOLD
DIGGERS

Finding the Gold in Every Person

PAULA TROW

GOLD
DIGGERS

Finding the Gold in Every Person

REDEMPTION
PRESS

© 2020 by Paula Trow. All rights reserved.

Published by Redemption Press, PO Box 427, Enumclaw, WA 98022.

Toll-Free (844) 2REDEEM (273-3336)

Redemption Press is honored to present this title in partnership with the author. The views expressed or implied in this work are those of the author. Redemption Press provides our imprint seal representing design excellence, creative content, and high-quality production.

No part of this publication may be reproduced, stored in a retrieval system, or transmitted in any way by any means—electronic, mechanical, photocopy, recording, or otherwise—without the prior permission of the copyright holder, except as provided by US copyright law.

Unless otherwise indicated, all Scripture quotations are taken from the New American Standard Bible® (NASB), Copyright © 1960, 1962, 1963, 1968, 1971, 1972, 1973, 1975, 1977, 1995 by The Lockman Foundation. Used by permission. www.Lockman.org

Scripture quotations marked NKJV are taken from the New King James Version. Copyright © 1982 by Thomas Nelson, Inc. Used by permission. All rights reserved.

Scripture quotations marked NIV are taken from the Holy Bible, New International Version®, NIV® Copyright ©1973, 1978, 1984, 2011 by Biblica, Inc.® Used by permission. All rights reserved worldwide.

Scripture quotations marked TPT are taken from The Passion Translation®. Copyright © 2017, 2018 by Passion & Fire Ministries, Inc. Used by permission. All rights reserved. ThePassionTranslation.com.

Scripture quotations marked ASV are taken from the American Standard Version (ASV), Public Domain.

ISBN: 978-1-64645-236-1 (Paperback)
978-1-64645-237-8 (ePub)
978-1-64645-238-5 (Mobi)

Library of Congress Catalog Card Number: 2020920668

CONTENTS

INTRODUCTION

Why would I title a book about seeking God something like *Gold Diggers*? Nowadays, when we think about a gold digger, we usually think of someone who's out to take advantage of another person or situation. Well, I want us to think about a miner, a person who digs deep in the earth to find treasure. We are going to learn to dig deep into God's Word and His person to find the ultimate treasure of relationship with Him.

Maybe the best thing about digging for gold in God's Word is that not only do we come to know Him better, but we come to know ourselves better too. We come to see ourselves as He sees us. We find the unique treasures He placed in us when He created us. With that knowledge comes excitement and deeper relationship with our great Creator. And with that excitement comes a desire to reach out and dig for gold in other people—to help them come to the same saving knowledge of Jesus Christ that we have found, so that they can find gold too.

That's the kind of gold digger I hope everyone who reads this book will become. Are you ready to do some mining with me?

In these last days, He has poured out His Spirit on all flesh (Acts 2:17; Joel 2:28). This seems to stamp a high value on every single person—God's will is that not even one person should perish. The road is narrow, and only a few find it on their own. That's why I believe it has always been God's plan to use us to reach others. Romans 10:15 tells us "how beautiful are the feet of those who bring good news." As we reach out and into the lives of others, we give His Spirit (who has already been poured out onto all flesh) the chance to move in such a way that we can know for certain it is Him. This move of His Spirit is His invitation into relationship.

When the King of Glory calls you to be His son or daughter, nothing you have done *qualifies* you for that relationship. It is His gift of grace. Neither can anything you have done *disqualify* you. Only His mercy gives you access. Only His blood can make you righteous. It will wash away your sin, justify you, and make you as clean as if you had never sinned against Him. When you choose to believe, you are then called a chosen one, because He already chose you. You were knitted by Him in your mother's womb. You were known by Him before the foundation of the world. You were pre-destined for an incredible purpose on your journey into eternity.

Remembering His sacrifice on the cross is where our passion for others is birthed. I would urge you to fix your gaze on Jesus Christ on the cross. There, we are born again. There, we realize our need for a savior, our need to be loved by the One who has loved us all along. He is our first love because He loved us first, and this is where true love is found. The cross of Jesus Christ is where we realize His love for the entire human race.

His magnificent act of sacrificial love demonstrated His passion for every human, so that no one need perish. There is not one—no, not one single person—He did not die to redeem.

To those who gaze long enough, the Holy Spirit imparts some of this extravagant passion from the cross into our hearts. Partaking of His passion on the cross is how we see with His eyes into the lives of others. He gives us a desire and longing for each person to be forgiven and loved. We become passionate about Him and His love, and with this passion, we share His gospel and His Spirit, and this moves us deeply into a lifetime of *digging for gold*. God's love is pure and so, so beautiful. When we know His heart from this passionate place, we become His *gold diggers*.

My prayer for you as you turn these pages is that you will come to see glimmers of gold, and that you will find the glow of treasure in each day that the Lord has made. Rejoice and be glad in it! Indeed, He will fill you with gladness in His presence, as surely as He makes known to you His ways and as your life increases in the knowledge of Him. Inside His heart, you will experience an implosion of His love that you cannot contain.

I have found that His lovingkindness consumes me as I desire to know Him more each day. When I stay with my heart turned toward His, I realize more clearly that my purpose for living is to love, to *be* love. This becomes possible as I experience His nature.

I'm digging for treasure in the depths of God's heart, His pure heart of gold, and I want you to join me. Each day is another invitation to go deeper. His love is an absolute, endless treasure, and we are transformed into *gold diggers* only in this place. As He changes our nature, we begin to display His attributes because we've been with Him. Each day, we become more like Him. And as His *gold diggers*, we can reach into the lives of others, believing He created us all in His image and likeness.

CHAPTER ONE

His Lovingkindness Knows No Boundaries

May it never be that I would boast, except in the cross of our Lord Jesus Christ, through which the world has been crucified to me, and I to the world.
Galatians 6:14

I grew up without an understanding of how interested and intimate God is toward us. I never knew how much He desired to show us His love, His lovingkindness. But as I matured in my relationship with Him, I began to see His hand working directly in my life, and I realized He really was there, all the time, just waiting for me to invite Him to be involved. Many times, I would be in worship, in a place of desiring to know His heart, when I would hear or see things suddenly as if He had just dropped them into my mind.

I'd like to share one of those times with you. My daughter and son-in-law were stationed in Tennessee for a couple of years while he served in the army. I traveled to see them quite often from Florida. They were living in a townhome during this time, and my daughter had become acquainted with her next-door neighbor. The neighbor had clearly declared that she was not a believer; in fact, she claimed to be an atheist. She was a single mom of three, living with her boyfriend, pregnant again, and battling an addiction to smoking. Anxiety was wearing her down.

I was spending time in worship when the Lord brought her to my mind. I specifically saw a jar of peanut butter and some baked brownies. I immediately understood that I was to take these two things to her as a gift. I also knew that He would be faithful to present His message through me for her as He had previously done for others.

So the next day, I knocked on her door with my gift. I began talking to her about Jesus and how much He loves her, but she quickly interrupted to say that she was an unbeliever. She was strong in what she proclaimed until I told her about the peanut butter and brownies. Her eyes filled with tears, and she looked as if she had seen a ghost.

"I have been eating peanut butter by the spoonful," she said, "and I've been craving brownies for days but haven't felt like making any."

My eyes filled with tears too, as I told her how I often hear our Father's heart on behalf of others and share His deep passion to draw them unto Himself. God had also shared with me that He had been misrepresented in her life, both through her own mother's perspective of Him and through various religious beliefs. She allowed me to tell her about His love and redemption that day, and she listened.

There is nothing more beautiful than speaking God's amazing grace into someone's life. I call this *gold digging*! Of course it's seed planting, but it's also digging for gold inside the heart of a person who has no idea they can be loved the way God loves them. I believe that, in these precious intimate moments, the Holy Spirit is there, hovering over the person, waiting for the moment of belief as they are given the opportunity to believe the gospel they are hearing.

What is the gospel? Him—Jesus, on that cross—offering a way for that sinner to be reconciled to a Father who has loved them from the beginning of time but whom they have never known. What a privilege we've been given. What an honor. What a blessing.

A little more of that story . . .

That night as I prayed for my daughter's neighbor, I had a vision of blue baby blocks that spelled out "baby boy." Then I heard the Lord say, "He is going to be okay."

The following day, I saw her outside and she told me she had just gotten back from the doctor. She'd learned she was having a boy but there were some complications with the placenta. I shared more about our Father, His love, and what I had heard in my heart the night before.

I saw her again a couple days later, and she said, "I just want you to know that I've decided to go to church on Sunday." I think back about the tears that filled her eyes as the Holy Spirit moved in her as truth. His love was digging for gold inside her heart.

Why did John call himself the one "whom Jesus loved" (John 21:7)? He had so much confidence in this that *he called himself* the beloved. John laid his head on the chest of Jesus and lingered there at His heart. We can have the same confidence. Lingering allows Jesus to love us—to really love us—in the intimate way that we were created for. It's in this place of lingering and lounging on Jesus's heart that He draws us into knowing Him.

It is impossible to love Him without knowing Him, and it's impossible to know Him without spending time with Him. Every believer must come to a place for themselves of choosing to believe His Word and then going after Him. Reading His magnificent promises alone is not enough. We must press into Him, asking the Holy Spirit for help to know and believe through revelation of His person. It's by our continual choice that the person of Jesus is revealed.

He will never leave or forsake us once we choose to believe in Him, but the depth of the revelation we have of Him is dependent on us. As we draw near to Him, He draws near to us.

When we choose to seek God, we are on the road to finding fulfillment for every desire we've ever had. How? Because every longing, suppressed or acknowledged, is found in knowing Him. Around every corner of the journey to knowing Him is an intimate encounter with our intentional Creator. How marvelous are His light and His lovingkindness that draw us evermore close as we choose to believe, even when it sometimes seems too good to be true.

At some point, we should stop in our tracks and say, "God! You say I am to love You with all my heart, all my mind, and all my soul. But I must know You to love You. You know that, so You sent Your Son to die for me, so that the mysteries could be revealed. You did that for me!"

He also says we have been given the mind of Christ. We are no longer far from Him, and if He seems far from us, then we have not positioned ourselves to receive Him, to receive the revelation that will transform our minds. Our Father of Light is Spirit, and to know Him, we must choose to believe, to set out on this supernatural journey into His heart.

Many times we've heard that we must repent to be saved; we must repent to achieve breakthrough; we must repent and be sorry for our sins. To sinful people, this often seems difficult or undesirable. But repentance comes naturally when we choose to believe. Believing leads to seeking; seeking leads to finding; finding leads to knowing; and knowing leads to loving. Every bit of repentance ever needed comes as a natural result of being in His magnificent light. His being, His divine nature, His lovingkindness, and His pure intentions toward us cause sin to fall to the wayside as we choose to know Him.

When Jesus displayed His passion on the cross, He issued the invitation for all flesh. On that cross, He made a way for us and crushed every religion that demands works as a way for salvation.

Our salvation began when He died. Now, when we believe, our lives begin. Our spirits become one with our Creator. As we choose Him in relationship and renew our minds in Him daily, emptying ourselves of the traditions of men, we become aware of His presence. His presence fills all and is in all. When we live this way, we find ourselves continually having *ah-ha!* moments in awe of His love and intimate interactions with us.

As we draw closer, we gain new awareness of Him. We begin seeing through His eyes, not just our own. We hear with ears that only hear His voice. We speak what the Father speaks. We taste His goodness, and we touch others with the gentleness of the Lamb that was slain. And all of that will lead us to reach into the hearts of others, looking for gold.

Experiencing Him is life. It brings unspeakable joy. Our great Creator God has given each of us the power of our own free will. It's in our choosing to believe that we give His Spirit our attention for Him to move, to teach, to comfort, to reveal. But it's the choosing to yield to His powerful and all-consuming Holy Spirit that changes our lives.

When our choosing leads to believing and then to yielding, moments of revelation begin. His love and personage become real, and a passionate love story begins. That story has no end . . . it is a circle of love. The gold digging seems to happen naturally, cyclically. Jesus digs and reveals to us who He created for us to be as we dig inside His heart to reveal hidden mysteries. Then as our lives change, we become *gold diggers* in others, in the most unsuspecting lives—even strangers we meet on the street. When God's lovingkindness flows through our hearts, it knows no boundaries.

CHAPTER TWO

Reach Out

The promise is for you and your children and all who are
far off, as many as the Lord our God will call to Himself.
Acts 2:39

I passed him on the side of the road; he was dangerously close to the busy highway. I stopped and drove back to him. By the time I approached, he had fallen face down in the dirt. I got on my knees and asked, "Are you okay?"

He looked at me and said, "I'm just drunk."

I placed my hand on his shoulder and felt the power of the Holy Spirit touch him. I said, "Jesus loves you. He loves you so much."

The man began to weep uncontrollably. A police officer had also stopped and now asked me to leave. The man had his wallet and was not homeless. Perhaps he was just hopeless. I was able to give him what his heart needed to hear and what his spirit needed to experience—the powerful love of the living God who sees *gold* in every person.

Will you dig for Him today? We often think there must be more to sharing God's love than simply reaching out to someone, but there doesn't have to be. In our culture, we find it uncomfortable to invade someone else's space. We consider it weird to offer to pray for a stranger. We're taught not to reach out and touch those we don't know. But people are hurting, and they need Jesus.

The gospel is simple: Jesus loves people.

Knowing God's heart enables us to hear what He is saying. Knowing how He feels about someone comes from hearing His passionate call to draw them closer. Spending time with Him and choosing to live a life abiding with Him changes us. His presence awakens who we are created to be. Then our eyes see every person with sincere passion; we become His mouthpiece, desperately calling them out of the darkness and into God's marvelous light. Knowing His heart imparts to us the same longing He has to draw each person into His eternal life. He loves us with an everlasting love and draws us with lovingkindness.

It's important for us to remember that as we reach out and into people's lives, we are being the hands and feet of Jesus—the Holy Spirit's love living inside of us is Jesus Himself calling people to Himself. We are His representatives throughout the earth now, and we should reach out with the exact same message Jesus was reaching out with on the cross. It is those people we see being the most hurtful to others who are the ones who need Him the most.

My husband and I were out for breakfast one morning, and I overheard a woman talking to her granddaughter while we were all waiting to be seated. The granddaughter was only about three years old, and I had heard some terribly hurtful things the grandmother had said. I was moved toward the heart of the grandmother as the Holy Spirit began to reveal some things about her own life: she had fallen so far away from Him as the demands of full-time tending to the needs of grandbabies was wearing heavy on her.

Once we were all seated at our own tables, I felt drawn to go over to her. I knelt down beside her and just started talking. I asked her if I could lay my hand on her arm. She was just staring at me as I told her that her Lord Jesus misses spending time with her on her front porch—this was something she had stopped doing a long time ago. She looked at me and said, "You have no idea what you've just said to me. You have no idea what this means to me." But the interesting thing is, I do know—I do know because I know His love and how very intentional He is.

We can begin reaching out by just being intentional, just like Jesus. Then along the way, we start to hear His whispers for people, words of knowledge from His very heart. But the reaching-out part can be so simple, and the Holy Spirit powerfully moves in our own hearts in these times because as we reach out and love, He is reaching in, digging in to our hearts and again bringing out treasures of gold.

CHAPTER THREE

What If?

*We are taking every thought captive
to the obedience of Christ.*
2 Corinthians 10:5

What if we took captive every thought that came into our minds that did not align with how Jesus looks at, feels about, or thinks about someone? What if we decided to intentionally take captive every thought that does not speak His truth? What if we took those thoughts captive to the obedience of Christ?

What is the obedience of Christ? Isn't it Him crucified? Isn't it Him passionately crying out to our Father in heaven, saying, "Father, forgive them for they do not know what they are doing" (Luke 23:34)? "For God so loved the world, that He gave His only begotten Son, that whoever believes in Him shall not perish, but have eternal life" (John 3:16). We who believe in Him should follow Him in obedience.

So what if His children became strategic in the war, realizing the war is not against flesh? Second Corinthians 10:5 says we should be "destroying speculations and every lofty thing raised up against the knowledge of God, and we [should be] taking every thought captive to the obedience of Christ." Ephesians 6:12 explains that "our struggle is not against flesh and blood but against the rulers, against the powers, against the world forces of this darkness, against the spiritual forces of wickedness in the heavenly places."

What if we turned on the evening news with a purpose of *digging for gold* in the worst person on the news that day? The child molester. The mother who beat her child to death. The elementary school teacher who was found with child pornography on his computer. What if we took that information captive on behalf of those persons and interceded for them *because our war is not against them*? When we become strategic in this way, it changes our nature. When we choose to take our thoughts captive unto what Jesus has done to redeem every person, that's when we will find the Holy Spirit working in our own hearts, changing us to be more like Him. Taking our free will and choosing His Word over the most heart-wrenching sin in this world opens the way for our heavenly Father to crush the enemy.

Our prayers are powerful. That's why we must choose His plan of redemption for each person we intercede for in our prayers, even those we do not know personally. When we do, our Father sends angels to minister into those lives, to move them toward salvation. Interceding for them in prayer also opens our hearts to hear the Father's voice concerning them. And He is a miracle-working God. We can pray the boldest prayers for those the world says are unworthy and throwaways, and when we do, our King Jesus may whisper His plan for them in our ears.

Isaiah 55:8–9 tells us, "'My thoughts are not your thoughts, nor are your ways My ways,' declares the LORD. 'For as the heavens are higher than the earth, so are My ways higher than your ways and My thoughts than your thoughts.'"

Without Jesus, that's where we're stuck. We cannot know the mind of God. But Jesus came to give us His thoughts—"For who has known the mind of the LORD that He will instruct Him? *But we have the mind of Christ*" (1 Corinthians 2:16, emphasis mine). Isn't that exciting?

A heart postured to be changed by Him, will be. As we dig for the gold in God's heart, He changes us to reflect His nature. This is what true love does. The person of God changes our nature. And as we find His gold, He calls it forth in us. And we in turn call out the gold in others. This is part of God's refining process.

In Zechariah 13:9, God tells us, "I will . . . refine them as silver is refined, and test them as gold is tested. They will call on My name, and I will answer them; I will say, 'These are My people'; and they will say, 'The LORD is my God.'" Now, some people say this Scripture is only talking about the trials we walk through. But I think our spiritual growth is part of the refining too. After all, to love like Him is the goal.

Learning to love the unlovable is a process of walking through the fire. We have been taught to go after justice against those who have committed great sin. If we're looking through Jesus's eyes, however, we will see them through mercy. To do that, we must again choose to take captive the traditions of men, the thoughts that are against the knowledge of the crucified Christ. This is our Father's war, and He has already won it. His justice crushes the enemy under our feet as we lift the highest praise to Him with these things that we choose not to war against in the flesh. Choosing His truth is giving Him praise. *We bring Him great joy by choosing His word and truth about someone's life.* His passion becomes our passion.

Every breath we have is an opportunity to believe every word He has ever said and is saying. We must use every breath that we are given to speak life into those around us. After all, "death and life are in the power of the tongue" (Proverbs 18:21).

We live in a dangerous world, and many of us worry that we can't go anywhere and feel safe. It's been said that the enemy has stolen our freedom of even going to the gas station safely. But *what if?* What if we became strategic in our everyday lives? What if we planned our trips to the gas station and the grocery store as strategic opportunities to bless someone?

Matthew 16:18 says "the gates of Hades will not overpower

[God's people; the church]." As dark as a place may seem, light still shines in darkness. Be that light. Do not hide your light under a basket—step out and be bold with His love. The Holy Spirit gives us the power to do all He has called us to do, and He has called us to love our neighbor. Our neighbor is not only the person who lives next door. Our neighbor is the grumpy person at the gas station too. Give Jesus away. Not by simply doing a good deed—there are others doing good deeds just to mark it off their checklist of being a good citizen. Good deeds do not change the world.

Love—the original love who is Jesus—is the world changer, atmosphere alterer, and heaven shaker. The righteousness of God cannot be separated from the love of God, and His love cannot be separated from His righteousness. One without the other is false religion. But the two together present the all-consuming fire of the Lord that will break and crush every form of evil.

Humanly speaking, this all seems impossible. Our hearts don't desire to love like this. But this is why our lives as Christians must be firmly rooted inside the person of Jesus, where our spirits are unified with Him as one, "for God has not given us a spirit of timidity, but of power and love and discipline" (2 Timothy 1:7). And with that, He also gave us an official mandate to do something—that mandate is to *love*.

We're all familiar with 1 Corinthians 13, the chapter that describes how we should love. I like to read it in the Passion Translation. Its fresh language makes me look more carefully at its instruction.

> Love is large and incredibly patient. Love is gentle and consistently kind to all. It refuses to be jealous when blessing comes to someone else. Love does not brag about one's achievements nor inflate its own importance. Love does not traffic in shame and disrespect, nor selfishly seek its own honor. Love is not easily irritated

or quick to take offense. Love joyfully celebrates honesty and finds no delight in what is wrong. Love is a safe place of shelter, for it never stops believing the best for others. Love never takes failure as defeat, for it never gives up.

Love never stops loving. It extends beyond the gift of prophecy, which eventually fades away. It is more enduring than tongues, which will one day fall silent. Love remains long after words of knowledge are forgotten. Our present knowledge and our prophecies are but partial, but when love's perfection arrives, the partial will fade away. (1 Corinthians 13:4–10 TPT).

This is divine love. This love is the radiance and very nature of God, who is Spirit.

What if we chose to believe every day that we can know Him more by digging for gold inside His heart? I have found in my own life that as I take communion and remember Jesus on the cross, His body broken and His blood shed for me, I see His heart. I see that there is only love in this kind of sacrifice. I experience His love in intimate ways, as it touches places in my being that I had no idea even existed.

This intimate place of remembering Him on the cross has become a dwelling place for me. This is my life's most prized possession—this treasure I have found by dwelling at His feet beneath the cross. There, each day, He gives me a heart of gold. I believe, and in return I receive a ring of gold, a circle of love that is eternal, a love that nothing can destroy. A love divine, from which no trial or persecution that I endure can separate me. What an exchange!

CHAPTER FOUR

Believing

*For God so loved the world that He gave His only
begotten Son, that whoever believes in Him shall not
perish, but have everlasting life.*
John 3:16

"Whoever believes in Him . . ." The power of all things is held in that one word, *believe*. Who holds the power to believe? Every single person.

What—or who—makes believing so powerful? Our magnificent Creator.

He created us with the ability to choose with our own minds, with our own wills. Our magnificent Creator also supplied a fire starter for the moment we choose to believe. At the instant the gospel is presented to us, the Holy Spirit (who is poured out on all flesh) is there, ready to start the fire.

That God has given us the power to choose to believe is amazing. This realization should stop us for a bit. What does believing change? It opens the door to heaven coming to earth. Once we choose to believe in Jesus Christ, and we continue choosing to believe, life changes. With every breath that we choose Him, we can know that He has also chosen us.

In John 15:4, we read, "Abide in Me, and I in you. As the branch cannot bear fruit of itself unless it abides in the vine, so neither can you unless you abide in Me." To me, choosing to believe

Him continually is the abiding. "Abide in Me, and I in You." God's Word may seem too good to be true, but this is our Father giving us *all* the power over our own lives. Read it again: "Abide in Me, and I [will abide] in you." What this tells me is, if I choose every second of every day to abide in Him, then the almighty Rock of Ages will abide also in me.

Wait. This is too much. God, how? Are you sure? How can this be?

But it is true. He is moving mightily, even at this precise moment. Let Him move your heart to abide continually. This is His desire; this is His written Word. This is Him saying, *My will is for your will, to choose Me, and when you choose Me, I will never forsake you. I will give you all of who I am in every moment.*

How different would our lives be if we took our power to choose to believe for what it is—the most powerful thing He could have ever given us? The simplicity of it is exciting. We have made it so difficult, but the simplicity is in the choosing. When we choose Him, He starts the transformation. As we continue to choose Him, He continues to draw us with His lovingkindness. We choose Him again, and His grace becomes evident in our lives. We choose Him; He moves. This is the life cycle with our Father. As we abide in Him—He abides in us.

I am so fascinated by Him, because the more I look for Him, the more I see Him and the more I believe in what He wants to do. It's an incredibly amazing life to live in expectancy of Him. He is so much more than we have dreamed. Let's choose to believe and let our journey in Him become everything He died to give us.

For myself, it seems that the more I know His heart, the more childlike my faith becomes; what I believe is simple. Over and over as I choose to believe that He wants me to know Him intimately, I continue to find Him. I continue to see Him in all things, and with this childlike faith of believing, I continue to experience His presence. His presence is consuming me; my desire to know Him increases every day. As I look back over my journey with Him, I can see how He has changed me. His love draws me closer every moment I choose simply to believe. I *believe* that God loved the world so much that He gave His only Son, and I am *experiencing* everlasting life inside the heart of God. He has rooted me in the simple knowledge that His grace is His gift and His mercy is His character.

That knowledge enables me to see others with a belief that deep inside each person, there is gold waiting to be refined, because *every person* has the God-given ability to choose to believe in Him. And this simple choice of believing, for every person who does, opens the door for us to enter in.

Nothing hinders us from becoming His gold diggers when we choose to live in this simple belief: Jesus came because He loves the world.

CHAPTER FIVE

Human Nature or Divine Nature?

*May the Lord direct your hearts into the love of God and
into the steadfastness of Christ.*
2 Thessalonians 3:5

Imagine you have some special friends coming over for dinner, and you know in advance how hungry they will be. You love them very much, and you want to share with them the best of what you have. So you pull out everything you have and prepare for them a beautiful meal. But when they come to dinner, they eat only a little of what you have prepared. "Oh, no," they say. "This is enough." Others said they were hungry but chose not to come at all to the lavish table that you prepared.

This is what it is like when we choose not to partake in all that the Father has prepared for us. He has given us Jesus—His everything!—so we could come and eat at His table of divine glory. Yet I have heard many say that what they have of Him is enough. They choose to believe there is no more to eat, or they choose to believe that in some way, wanting to have more is being ungrateful for what they've already received.

The truth is that He has given and prepared for us so much more than we are aware of. Our desire to partake of all He has prepared for us should grow more intense each day—and it will, as we become one with Him.

Every time we choose Him, we are transformed a little more

into the very nature of God. He created us in His image, and it is His heart's longing to bring us back to His original plan. I believe His original plan was for us to experience life without the knowledge of any evil thing. In the beginning we were commanded by God to not eat of the tree of the knowledge of good and evil. It was His will for us to walk with Him and to know Him, just like Adam and Eve had done. But their sin separated us from that plan.

Now, because Jesus has come to make the way back to the garden of life possible, we can trade in or "trade up" our human nature for His divine nature. Once again, Christ crucified is proof of His longing and passion for us. "God created man in His own image, in the image of God He created him; male and female He created them" (Genesis 1:27).

This is our daily bread. This is the table He has set for us. It is Jesus. As we take and eat and choose and yield, we trade our human nature for His divine nature. Worship and adoration for Him becomes our life's song, our life's reason, and we long to know Him more and more. We long to become as passionate for Him as He has always been for us.

At times, it seems impossible, as we live our lives in this world, to experience His presence continually. It's as if we have been trained to separate and categorize our lives. But this is not His will. This is the manipulation and deception of evil. It has snuck in through the traditions of men, and it has led to gross unbelief. We find ourselves quoting Scripture in such nonchalant ways. We say, "I can do all things through Christ who strengthens me" (Philippians 4:13 NKJV). We also say, "If God is for us, who can be against us?" (Romans 8:31 NKJV).

But what if we chose to actually, actively, believe what we say we believe? We would become world changers with every word we speak, instead of people who simply quote Scripture. I think for myself that the simplicity of this thing is what makes it so difficult accept. I have tried to make it more complicated in my own life a thousand times. But when I surrender my ways, my own attempts to understand—that's when I find Him again and again.

As I learn to give up my selfish desire to be "good enough," I experience the grace and love that comprise His divine nature. He gives me the gift of renewing my mind, and all He asks of me is to continue believing. This mystery unfolds daily in my heart—Christ loving me extravagantly, intentionally, even as He lives inside me, actively transforming the very nature of who I once was into His own image.

It's true! We can partake of His nature and become one with the magnificent Father of all creation. His Spirit is extravagantly intoxicating, and once we have tasted and once we have seen Him, we continually desire more. Partakers are world changers. We are the *gold diggers.* "O taste and see that the LORD is good; how blessed is the man who takes refuge in Him!" (Psalm 34:8). And also "For by these, He has granted to us His precious and magnificent promises, so that by them you may become partakers of the divine nature, having escaped the corruption that is in the world by lust" (2 Peter 1:4).

Choosing Him—and making up our own minds to do so constantly—brings a heightened awareness of Him. It becomes so intense that we truly have moments throughout the day when we experience His magnificent presence so powerfully that His joy permeates our being. This is the authentic power and purpose of the Holy Spirit! Every day we can wake up so aware of Him that we hear the song He is singing over us! "Jehovah thy God is in the midst of thee, a mighty one who will save; he will rejoice over thee with joy; he will rest in his love; he will joy over thee with singing" (Zephaniah 3:17 ASV).

In John 17, we get a glimpse of Jesus speaking to the Father. "You are my righteous Father," He says, "but the unbelieving world has never known you in the perfect way that I know you! And all those who believe in me also know that you have sent me! I have revealed to them who you are, and I will continue to make you even more real to them, so that they may experience the same endless love that you have for me, for your love will now live in them, even as I live in them!" (John 17:25–26 TPT).

Jesus Himself said that the unbelieving world has never known the Father like He knows the Father. But now, *those who believe in Him* will experience the same love that Jesus experiences from the Father. This is the gold! Jesus promised to continue to make our Father in heaven more real to us. What an amazing promise He has given!

It seems to me that our believing is the digging, and our digging is the partaking of His divine nature.

CHAPTER SIX

Counterfeit Emotions

If you continue in My word, . . . you will know the truth,
and the truth will make you free.
John 8:31–32

All too often, when we stop to examine ourselves, we find that our emotions have been connected to a counterfeit source. The ruler of this world deceives us in this area more than any other. We've allowed him to stream lies and deceit into our minds. From there, his deceptions flow through our thoughts to our emotions and result in selfish ambition. Selfish ambition touches every area of our lives, it sneaks in through the emotion of entitlement, and we find ourselves entertaining self-centeredness as the answer to our heart's cries.

But Jesus restores us back to our divine source, so that our emotions are again spiritually fueled from our Creator. God created us with emotions, intending that His living water would flow through us. When our emotions are fueled by His streams of living water, we live in His image as compassionate, loving, and forgiving people. No one is held responsible for our happiness, because our Father God fills our emotions with His divine love. This was His plan.

We will never grasp the full breadth or depth of the expanse of His heart. We could not take hold of all He is or comprehend the vastness of His love—yet this eternal King continues knocking at the door of every heart.

The enemy loves to condemn us, to trick our minds into believing his lies. Chains of condemnation trap us in a mindset of unworthiness, and the walls of our own minds become the very prison that holds us captive. We tend to think on the side of logic—we believe the things that make sense to us. This is where fear rules, but we don't have to stay there. Our relationship with the Holy Spirit is the guiding light into all things that are possible with God. The Holy Spirit highlights and celebrates truth continually.

Those who believe that God and Satan are equals have listened to the lies of the devil. We who know the Father know that Satan is nothing more than a created being of our incredibly vast God. In the presence of the Living One who breathes life and *is* life, Satan himself is no more than a vapor. He has no substance or power there.

We become dangerous to Satan's plans when we choose to believe Him who is Truth—Jesus Christ. Believing Him for ourselves eventually leads us to long for every person we meet to come to this saving knowledge of Jesus Christ. This is where *gold diggers* are born—in the place of freedom and truth. "So if the Son makes you free, you will be free indeed" (John 8:36). "This is good and acceptable in the sight of God our Savior, who desires all men to be saved and to come to the knowledge of the truth" (1 Timothy 2:3–4).

I have heard it said (and preached) that God never said that He wants us to be happy. I would say that if there is truth in that, it is only because happiness cannot contain the fullness of His joy being made complete inside us. His joy is so great, so immense. It can reach and penetrate even the greatest of human heartache.

The remedy for a heart that believes this lie of unhappiness is found in a visit to His feet. Our visitations there become a place where we linger and behold the Lamb of God who held nothing back in order to give us everything. His passion becomes alive in us through our embrace. His joy—His *exceeding* joy—comes as an explosion within our souls. It overwhelms us in a way that happiness cannot do.

But how can a dying world believe in a gospel that so many of us have no joy in expressing? We must allow His love—this love we say we believe in—to flow through us to the world.

So often we seek Jesus for peace. We will always find it in Him, but He is so much more than that! His character is the fullness of God. He is so kind, and the more I get to know Him, I realize how lighthearted He is. He's never in a hurry—He has no need to be. Eternity is at His command. He offers peace at its fullest. Peace from Jesus is steadfast, longsuffering, gentle, playful, and never accusing or belittling.

Jesus is the most amazing person. He is lighthearted yet full of all the weightiness of glory. He's playful with childlike simplicity yet His glorious being shines brighter than the sun. We were created to behold Him with reverence, all the while experiencing the exuberance of all He offers—the fullness of God. When we are in relationship with Him, the very person of peace becomes our emotional resource. His living water is from the deepest well, a well of divine life that is eternally ours. This eternal revelation of Jesus as our Prince of Peace is where we come alive again and again.

Our emotions were created by Him to be resourced by Him. As peace becomes our source, His ways and nature become our evidence. As our emotions display steadfast trust through any trial, His living joy shines through our lives.

Knowing Him is being loved by Him. The full circle of His love is so intriguing. He commands us to love Him, and so we follow those who have built ideas around what they think loving God means. But really, He is simply saying, *Come to Me; get to know Me.* When He commanded us to love Him, He knew that loving Him would bring us every desire of our heart. But we, in our natural minds, twist that command into a militant lifestyle of striving to do good, and we miss the promise that our Father has given to us, that loving Him brings unspeakable joy through the blissful partaking of His being. Oh, He is so much more than just a good Father!

Jesus said, "'YOU SHALL LOVE THE LORD YOUR GOD WITH ALL YOUR HEART, AND WITH ALL YOUR SOUL, AND WITH ALL YOUR MIND.' This is the great and foremost commandment" (Matthew 22:37–38). Commanding us in this way was His way of bringing to us life everlasting. His love is truly remarkable. When we make the effort to know Him, we learn that time spent with Him is the most valuable time of all.

God's Word is filled with absolutes for us to take hold of with our hearts. We must believe these truths fully, not just memorize them. We've all known people who can quote Scripture effortlessly. We may even have been impressed by this, only to be sadly disappointed when we saw what unfolded in their lives later on. Memorizing for the sake of quoting Scripture does not cause the renewing transformation we are promised. Words repeated from the head and not the heart lead only to a life that continues to look like the world.

But when we choose to believe His Word, when we saturate our minds with His truth and long to really know Him, we find ourselves truly transformed by His Word. Our belief collides with the Holy Spirit, and He washes us with holy scriptures. We become living epistles. God has written it all on our hearts already, and everything Jesus said that would be brought back to our memory, will be.

It is the Holy Spirit's pleasure to reveal the secrets of Jesus to hearts diligently seeking to know Him. He has set eternity inside us. Something happens in those moments when we turn our hearts toward Him and desire to know Him. It's an exchange of sorts—as we desire to love Him with all of who we are, He takes our un-belief and replaces it with His presence, and that draws us into wanting to know Him more. Our thoughts and emotions toward others are changed in ways that can only be described as divine. As we become connected to our source of life, all our emotions are grounded in His peace, a steadfast reminder that our old life is renewed by the power of the Holy Spirit, revealing to us the new life we now have in Christ.

CHAPTER SEVEN

Reflections on Joy

You will make known to me the path of life; in Your presence is fullness of joy; in Your right hand there are pleasures forever.
Psalm 16:11

For many years, I thought the word "joy" was just a church word. Church people used the word, but rarely did I hear anyone talk about it in a way that interested me. Few people evidenced this joy they spoke of. They were just ordinary people with everyday struggles. No, *joy* was only a church word—I was sure of it.

But there was one lady I will never forget—a Sunday school teacher who was always smiling. Her smile was different from everyone else's. She was strangely kind, almost weird. I'd never experienced someone quite like her before. I remember her mentioning that she prayed for each of us while on her knees before the Lord. She just *talked* to Him about us. She talked so much about spending time in prayer, but I thought it was odd to pray by yourself to a God who felt so far away. Where was He, anyway?

Everyone at church said that He was alive and that He lived inside us. But if that was true, why did we look the same as the rest of the world? Why did we hurt other people and get upset with each other for this or that? I was growing up in a church, experiencing church people using church words, but not experiencing Him.

As a teenager, I tried to read my Bible, and I do believe I was saved. I knew something inside me was different than others who weren't Christians. But the Bible just didn't make sense, especially when I read about joy. I didn't understand what it meant when I read about being "full of Christ" and loving others. It was as if my church was filled with people who used words from the Bible, but their lives were far from showing real evidence or meaning of those words. It also seemed strange that there were so many promises in the Bible about healing and loving and, again, that word *joy*.

It was crazy to me that every single rule these church people were so concerned about holding each other accountable to was supposedly made in the name of love. They talked about love and worked hard to show each other love, but was it real or just a rule? If someone was sick or in the hospital, somebody from church made sure to visit them. If someone died, people from church would cook meals for the family. But sometimes I heard things like, "Well, we still have to love them, even when they make mistakes." Love seemed more like a chore, a rule, than anything else.

I grew up understanding about things that were sinful because we talked about it a lot. Deep inside, I believed those things were wrong and sinful too. But I was keenly aware of the hypocrisy of it all. Something was missing. There had to be some important key to this "victory in Jesus" that we sang about on Sunday mornings, and as far as I could tell, we didn't have it. So where was the victory in Jesus that could lead these people to what was missing?

What was missing?

As I got older, I went to church only sporadically. Occasionally, I read the Bible, but I lived a selfish life, deceived by the ways of the world. There was a big empty place inside me, but I didn't know I was looking to fill it. That's odd, I know, but it's true. I was looking out into the world, looking to other people, looking for anything to make me feel whole.

It took me a long time to understand that the void inside me was there for a purpose. It was created to be filled only by God

Himself. I was searching for love, but church had taught me that love was something I was supposed to do. I didn't know it was a person I could know.

The emptiness I was walking around with had been there so long, I thought it was just a normal thing. I had no reason to think otherwise. But walking around empty caused me to make unwise decisions, sometimes at great cost. I lived selfishly, hurting myself and others while always finding a way to justify my actions. I was living by the ways of the world and leaving a blood trail behind me as I hurt the ones I thought were there to fill that empty place inside.

By the time I was in my early twenties, I was married for the second time and a stay-at-home mommy to three kids. My husband and children were everything to me. They filled the void—or so I thought. Until one day I started thinking about that word.

Joy.

As filled as I was with the love of my family, I knew I had not yet experienced joy. The word was so "churchy," yet something about it rang true to me. There had to be more to it, something that I had never understood. But that's just it—I didn't understand because joy is not meant to be understood, it is meant to be experienced.

So that day, I looked up to heaven and asked, "What is joy? How can it be better than this happiness that I know now?"

That night, I had a dream. In the dream, I was looking up to the clouds. They were drifting by beautifully, and as they moved, I saw the word "joy." Just as I saw the word, I experienced true joy. It was the most amazing thing. It was the most real, tangible experience in my soul that I had ever had. It was life changing. In just a few moments, I had experienced more than I ever had before in my life. My spirit experienced Him in a new way, and I was awakened to the reality of eternity for what felt like the very first time.

My belief to that point had been real—I was a Christian, and I knew that He had saved me. I believed in Jesus and knew I would spend eternity forever with Him. Essentially, He had been washing my sins daily, moment by moment as I lived in the world, but I was far from His heavenly places. My spirit had not yet been awakened to the reality of His kingdom in my life.

But in that one moment, I was changed. When my heart turned toward His and I asked Him about joy—my heart to His heart— He came and awakened my spirit. He wanted a relationship with me, and I wanted a relationship with Him.

I finally had my answer.

When our eyes are opened to life in the Spirit, we are changed forever by His invitation to come close and enter in. This is joy.

Joy was what was missing for so many at my church all those years ago. Joy is what made my Sunday school teacher different. She had joy that comes from time spent in secret with the secret teller.

Only He can awaken us and fill the void that He placed in us. He touches us throughout our lives—in a song at church, through an act of kindness someone shows us, or through an unexpected blessing that could only be from Him. These are invitations for us to come closer, to get to know Him. *He is the joy!* He is found for each of us personally, in secret. Time spent with Him secretly and privately leads to an awakened, joy-filled life. Our relationship with Him should be one of joy.

We should not live this life with just one experience of Him. That first experience of Him touching our hearts, the moment that moved us to receive Him as our Savior—it was never meant to sustain our Christian walk with Him. The moments throughout our lives are invitations to come closer, to know Him intimately, to interact regularly, not just to remember times when He touched us in a certain way. These moments are significant and life changing, but we must take hold of the invitation. It is His pleasure to bring joy to us this way.

We often ask Him for blessings when we take the time to pray. And He invites us to dig for the treasure there. But He gets great joy when our hearts are positioned to experience His joy for ourselves. This truly is His passion, for us to know Him and be filled continually by Him alone with exceeding joy. "For you make him most blessed forever. You make him joyful with gladness in your presence" (Psalm 21:6).

CHAPTER EIGHT

Our Significant Lives

Before I formed you in the womb, I knew you,
and before you were born, I consecrated you.
Jeremiah 1:5

D o you realize that you have an extraordinarily significant life to live—one designed and completely personalized by our wonderful Father? The moment *we choose* to be His, we become *His chosen* children. Each one of us individually brings joy to the heart of our Father.

Are you aware of the special place you hold in His heart? It is a place reserved for only you, a place that no one else can touch. There is not one other person in all of time and creation who could offer the joy your worship brings to His heart. There is no other person who can fulfill the destiny He has planned for your life. He longs to use your life.

God has a plan for every person who has or will live on this earth. We were created to bring His kingdom to earth. And we were predestined to love Him.

As we remember the cross again and again, let us remember that we are the joy that was set before Him as He endured that sacrifice. And now, when we choose to be His, we are His reward.

How intimately is He concerned about us? In Psalm 56:8, we read, "You have taken account of my wanderings, put my tears in Your bottle. Are they not in your book?" It is so special to know that "the very hairs of your head are all numbered" (Matthew 10:30; Luke 12:7). He doesn't just know *how many* hairs are on our heads; each one has a number. Every hair, imagine! "Do not fear; you are more valuable than many sparrows" (Luke 12:7). And one more comfort is, "Behold, I have inscribed you on the palms of My hands; your walls are continually before Me" (Isaiah 49:16). How incredibly mysterious is that?

These things that are written must change our way of thinking about our Father God in such a way that it's impossible for our lives to look the same. We must believe His written Word. It is a love letter, an invitation for an intentional journey into the depths of His heart.

His righteousness could and should be the death of us, but through His amazing grace, it is instead the power that lives in us, giving us tremendous victory over every evil thing. His righteousness is the holy purifier that can burn away every bit of rubbish in our lives.

He is gracious and so very longsuffering. His patience is the evidence of His desire for His children to ask and choose His will. When we ask for more of Him and His presence, He delights in pouring over us His glory, His holiness, and His righteous, loving fire. A heart that yearns to know Him will experience Him in ways that at times could seem too much. The weight of His glory is overwhelming. Yet, at the same time, it is the most exhilarating love we could ever imagined. This cannot be explained, only experienced.

Have you experienced His holiness? Have you given the Holy Spirit who lives in you permission to freely display His holiness in you? Make room for Him. Every knee will bow to Him on that day, but now we are called His righteousness. Should we not display Him? Demons should shudder, they should flee, they should bow to the Holy Spirit who is living inside us—and they will, as we become more like Him.

This is why we can live boldly, why we can walk into the darkest places: we know that His righteousness in us is the full armor of God. We are fully protected in Him, for His glory. As we draw near and experience His love for us, we begin to believe, to understand, that He was indeed strategic when He created us and that our lives are significant to His kingdom.

As a young person, I wanted the world to see me as someone important. It seemed a selfish desire at times, but now I realize it wasn't that at all. It was a deep longing to be loved by my heavenly Father, to know Him, and I wanted so much to understand my significance. Unfortunately, in my search for that significance, I filled my soul with the lusts of the world. I did not know that what I was so thirsty for was His holy fire to cleanse those unrighteous things from my life. When I finally surrendered, He began His work in me, cleansing me from impurity and making me whole and His. "He will baptize you with the Holy Spirit and fire. His winnowing fork is in His hand, and He will thoroughly clear His threshing floor; and He will gather His wheat into the barn, but He will burn up the chaff with unquenchable fire" (Matthew 3:11–12).

The Holy Spirit's purifying process has been painful at times, and yet it has filled me so profoundly with His love that I could not deny the significance of my life now in any way. His purifying fire does not leave ashes behind; instead, it reveals a love like no other and a heart that glistens with a refined gold that attracts heaven.

Our lives were the joy set before Him on the cross; for that reason, our lives are significant.

CHAPTER NINE

The Strength of a Mustard Seed

All things you ask in prayer, believing, you will receive.
Matthew 21:22

How much faith does it take to live this life of fullness I am speaking of—a fullness that reflects the very image of God?

It takes faith only the size of a mustard seed. God has already freely given to each person a measure of faith. He has pressed this tiny seed into the palm of your hand, but you must exercise your free will to claim it. Have you closed your hand and held on to it tightly, thereby proving just how little your faith is? Or have you decided to trust Him, believing that as you plant that tiny seed and seek His heart, that it will truly grow? I wonder if our ability to believe is an actual measure of faith that's been given to each of us. I also wonder if our ability to believe is the actual mustard seed Jesus was talking about to His disciples when He told them that's all that was needed—a mustard seed of faith. Maybe that's why He scolded them because He knew they each had been given the ability to have the faith they needed, and it was in the simplicity of choosing to believe.

Jesus said, "The kingdom of heaven is like a mustard seed, which a man took and sowed in his field; and this is smaller than all other seeds, but when it is full grown, it is larger than the garden plants and becomes a tree, so that the birds of the air come and nest in its branches" (Matthew 13:31–32).

We have the kingdom of heaven within us here on earth. Our faith brings the power of that kingdom down. We can contain it within ourselves as that tiny seed, or we can plant it and watch God do marvelous things. The disciples hadn't quite grasped this in Matthew 17—they had just failed at casting out some demons, and came to Jesus to ask why. Jesus responded, "Because of the littleness of your faith; for truly I say to you, if you have faith the size of a mustard seed, you will say to this mountain, 'Move from here to there' and it will move; and nothing will be impossible to you" (Matthew 17:20).

It seems as if Scripture cries out two distinct things in these passages, doesn't it? First it declares the enormity of God's love and passion for His children, then it points out our immense lack of belief. But Jesus knows our weakness, and He gave us Scripture for that too. In Mark 9, we see a young man, possessed by demons, and a father at his wits' end. The man begs Jesus "if You can" to help them. I can almost see Jesus, shaking His head: "And Jesus said to him, "'If You can?' All things are possible to him who believes.' Immediately the boy's father cried out and said, 'I do believe; help my unbelief'" (Mark 9:23–24).

All we need is a tiny mustard seed of faith. That's all! And because His Spirit has been poured out on all flesh, we each have an opportunity to believe. The moment we choose Him, He gives us our measure of faith. If *you* believe, *you* have faith! So what are you doing with what you have been given? You might feel like your faith is small or even like you have none at all, but He has given you a measure of it. Trust Him—let your tiny mustard seed grow into that flourishing tree He tells about in His Word.

In the same way Jesus says the kingdom of heaven is like a mustard seed, so is our relationship with Him. When we choose to believe the gospel and allow growth in our hearts, the kingdom of God becomes present in us. As we grow closer to Him, our tiny seed of faith flourishes into an amazing tree of life. His love stretches out through our wide-open arms. Because of our belief, many others will come to rest there, just as the birds of the air.

In the beginning, God placed Adam and Eve in the garden. The tree of life was at the center of it, and in the excellence of God's creation, everything was beautiful. Then Adam and Eve chose evil, and all of humanity was dismissed from the garden, from God's presence. But now, because of His grace and passion, Jesus says, "Take this mustard seed. If you believe and trust and seek Me and Me alone, the tree of life that was in that garden of Eden is Me in you and you in Me." What if we thought of our mustard seed as the very seed of the tree of life? I believe it is one and the same.

In Genesis 2:15, we read, "Then the LORD God took the man and put him in the garden of Eden to cultivate it and keep it." Since creation, it has been His heart to give us everything lovely and everything pure. He gives us rivers flowing with His peace because of His presence; He is the life-giving source that causes every drop to glisten.

"Now a river flowed out of Eden to water the garden; and from there it divided and became four rivers. The name of the first is Pishon; it flows around the whole land of Havilah, where there is gold" (Genesis 2:10–11). Adam and Eve were surrounded by His glory and beauty. But they chose evil over His goodness because their thoughts were influenced by the enemy who led them astray.

At times, each of us has been exposed to and witnessed just about every evil thing. Now, because of His grace and mercy, He says, "Will you choose Me? Will you choose to believe in My Son over evil?" His desire is our heart's yes.

So now, here we are in this world where evil has thrived, and we are offered this seed. Will we believe this tiny mustard seed can thrive and grow into the tree of life within us? Mustard seed faith is all it takes to live in the image of God—who He created us to be, died for us to be, resurrected for us to be, and then ascended for us to be. After all, "God created man in His own image, in the image of God He created him; male and female, He created them" (Genesis 1:27).

Maybe there's a reason a mustard seed looks a bit like gold—maybe this tiny seed of faith is actually the solid gold nugget we've already been given. This golden nugget of faith resides within each person. May we become the gold diggers reaching inside the hearts of others, helping them to find for themselves this tiny seed that can grow into the most wonderful tree of life.

CHAPTER TEN

Thanksgiving and Praise

*Enter His gates with thanksgiving
and His courts with praise.*
Psalm 100:4

We have been lulled to sleep by the dullness of the lies of the enemy, and Jesus is the only way for us to awake. The devil masquerades as an angel of light and has a counterfeit for all of God's glorious creation. In our deceived state, we think we know good. We think we know God. We think we know ourselves. But as we awaken from our sleep, like Jacob, we will say, "Surely, the LORD is in this place, and I did not know it. . . . How awesome is this place! This is none other than the house of God, and this is the gate of heaven."

We will no longer settle for the things of this world as seen through a dim light or as a glass half empty. Instead, we will see it all through the fullness and brightness of God, our eyes wide open to His glorious creation, filled with His presence. The Holy Spirit is here on this earth, and when the eyes of our spirits are opened, we live wide awake in wonder of our Creator who is in all things, fills all things, and who makes the old pass away. Once our spirits are awake, we become aware of all that He truly is. We experience life for the first time with each new breath because the illumination of His light is an all-consuming fire.

The power of life and death is in our tongue, and we can enter

His gates with thanksgiving and praise. What an amazing gift we have been given! We have the power to bless someone's life with our lips as we reign from His courts on high, seated with Him in the heavenly places. I tell you—we can live in that place with our Father. As we choose a heart postured toward the cross, our lips overflow with thanksgiving and praise. Heaven comes to earth, with angels ascending and descending from the throne of God. His kingdom comes as He inhabits our praises.

Jesus is knocking at our heart's door, but we must let Him in. Then, with Him inside us, our grateful hearts can enter those heavenly gates with no hesitation. The key to entering in is thankfulness. As we enter His gates with thanksgiving and His courts with praise, we begin to see all He has done. We begin making ourselves at home in this place of rejoicing. We learn who He is and know His ways.

If we hear a voice teaching, preaching, or proclaiming His character as anything other than love and passion for us, we can be certain that this is a false prophet because "the testimony of Jesus is the spirit of prophecy" (Revelation 19:10). The cross is the evidence and definition of passion. The cross belongs to Jesus Christ. Everything He's ever asked of us that requires obedience is so that our joy can be made complete in Him.

Every time He invites us to sacrifice something and we choose to be obedient, He meets our hearts in this new place, where uncharted waters become a place of serenity. Most of the time, we expect these sacrifices to be huge mountainlike decisions, as in giving everything away and moving to a third-world country, but He says simply, "offer to God a sacrifice of thanksgiving" (Psalm 50:14). This sacrifice is monumental. It holds the key to every breakthrough; it holds the key for every broken heart to be mended. Every time we don't understand what's going on around us in this world, our thanksgiving is a sacrifice.

What is a sacrifice of praise? It's when we choose to give up those emotions that define who we are, that influence our day-to-day lives, that determine whether we have a good or bad day, and we choose instead to praise God despite the circumstances around us. We choose with each moment and every breath to surrender these things—to sacrifice them—and we leave them behind as we enter His gates with thanksgiving, saying "This is the day which the LORD has made; let us rejoice and be glad in it" (Psalm 118:24). As we thank Him and choose to live in this place, He makes us new, bringing us back to His image. He is a good, good Father!

Thanksgiving and praise turn into a lifestyle of worship. The heart that is one with Him cannot be "undone" over anything except Jesus! Jesus becomes the filter for all things trying to enter our hearts or affect our emotions. *The* Prince of Peace longs to be *our* Prince of Peace. The still waters and green pastures we'll experience in the heavenly kingdom are the result of hearts that have sacrificed with thanksgiving and praise through rough seas and valleys.

Nothing moves God's heart more than our worship. The truth of His goodness becomes our biggest reality. We pray without ceasing from a place of gratefulness where we are amazed by who He is. To continually experience such awe-filled moments with Him is to be aware of His goodness. This realization is birthed through thanksgiving and realized at its fullness in a life dedicated to worship. We are true worshipers when we learn to love Him in truth and in spirit and as His heart continues to be revealed to us.

We experience true worship—in spirit and in truth—when there is no separation of our mind and spirit from Him. Heaven surrounds us with song, and the home we long for seems not so far away anymore. His kingdom comes. He is love, and we are His. "But an hour is coming, and now is, when the true worshipers will worship the Father in spirit and truth; for such people the Father seeks to be His worshipers. God is spirit, and those who worship Him must worship Him in spirit and truth" (John 4:23–24).

Psalm 100 brought a life-changing reality into my journey of knowing my Father in heaven. This instruction to enter His gates with thanksgiving and His courts with praise drew me further into His truth. As I became faithful to thank Him with my heart in every situation and praise Him continually, I realized that I no longer had room for ungratefulness. Even when I feel I have disappointed people in my life or when I don't understand certain circumstances, I can turn my heart to adore my Lord and Savior. As I remind myself of all that He's done, I find myself embraced by His presence because He faithfully inhabits my praise.

This has brought a new confidence to my relationship with Jesus, not because of anything I've done but because of His Word. I enter His gates and into His courts with faith, knowing that I belong there. I find myself proclaiming, "Better is one day in your courts than a thousand elsewhere" (Psalm 84:10 NIV). I don't quite know how to express the change my heart has gone through as I have found this amazing grace of God's love and experienced the victorious life Jesus offers.

When I think that He loves me, that He knows me, that He enjoys my company—my heart is filled with inexpressible joy, just as He promised. Even more remarkable is that no person, no created thing, no persecution, no trial, no demon, not even death can separate me from His love. My heart cannot stay silent. With the songwriter Isaac Watts, I proclaim, "Joy to the world; the Lord is come! Let earth receive her King!"

Have you experienced heavenly things? This is just a portion of the table He has prepared for you. Heaven is His kingdom coming and His will being done. I pray that you would, this very moment, make up your mind to enter His gates with thanksgiving and His courts with praise. I pray that you would choose to live in the freedom of His gift of grace, that you would turn your heart to adore Him in spirit and truth, and that you would believe that His mercy and goodness will follow you all the days of your life.

CHAPTER ELEVEN

Our Inheritance

*For we know that we will receive a reward, an
inheritance from the Lord, as we serve the Lord Yahweh,
the Anointed One!*
Colossians 3:24 tpt

It's impossible to pen all the things of the Holy Spirit. We can only encourage each other to choose Him and to dive into His ocean of unending eternal bliss. Oh, that we would enter in to receive the joy He has reserved for us!

We have allowed the phrase "joy comes in the morning" (Psalm 30:5) to become little more than a platitude that invites sorrow to stay a little longer. But a life lived inside His promises brings a complete fulfillment of our hearts' deepest desires. He fills us to overflowing and our cups run over. Our lives overflow with the abundance of His love. In Him, we can walk through a dry and thirsty land, leaving behind us streams of living water to spill over onto those around us. Our inheritance is for today! He is the bright and morning star who has come and is yet coming (Revelation 22:16).

There's so much more than platitude in Psalm 30:5. It is encouraging to me to know that "His anger is but for a moment, His favor is for a lifetime; weeping may last for the night, but a shout of joy comes in the morning." These aren't just nice words. They're solid reassurance of the inheritance we have in Christ. His anger was for a moment, but His favor is for a lifetime. He's our bright morning star; He turns our mourning and sorrows into joy. How amazing!

Many strive to do good, confessing along the way that all their treasures are stored up in heaven. But do we understand that Jesus *is* heaven? The very living Word of God is speaking to us, proclaiming that *He* is our treasure! *He* is the inheritance we read about in Colossians 3:24: "For we know that we will receive a reward, an inheritance from the Lord, as we serve the Lord Yahweh, the Anointed One" (TPT). There is hope in 1 Peter 1:3: "Celebrate with praises the God and Father of our Lord Jesus Christ, who has shown us his extravagant mercy. For his fountain of mercy has given us a new life—we are reborn to experience a living, energetic hope through the resurrection of Jesus Christ from the dead" (TPT). Then again in Ephesians 1:11: "Through our union with Christ we too have been claimed by God as his own inheritance. Before we were even born, he gave us our destiny; that we would fulfill the plan of God who always accomplishes every purpose and plan in his heart" (TPT).

This inheritance is spoken of many times in the Bible. Read with me again in 1 Peter 1:3–5, "According to His great mercy, [He] has caused us to be born again to a living hope through the resurrection of Jesus Christ from the dead, to obtain an inheritance which is imperishable and undefiled and will not fade away, reserved in heaven for you, who are protected by the power of God through faith for a salvation ready to be revealed in the last time." In Hebrews 11:6, we read that "without faith, it is impossible to please Him, for he who comes to God must believe that He is and that He is a rewarder of those who seek Him."

People speak about heaven as our destination after death, but it's so much more than that. Heaven is found in Christ alone, and He is our inheritance today! Today is the day for kingdom life to be revealed. Jesus's death entitles us to this inheritance now. The more we seek His heart; the more He is revealed to and in us. Tasting of this inheritance gives us a hunger for more, and as we fill our spirits by feasting on Him, we die to ourselves.

Feasting on the Lord leads to a life filled with all things lovely and pure. Feasting on the world leads to wanting more and more of things that will never satisfy. Constantly seeking and looking for the next best thing to quench a lustful heart leads only to a quicksand of emotional confusion. The world (the enemy) points us to dead-end streets that look promising at first but lead only to a chaotic nowhere. We are devoured as we run toward emptiness.

The world offers a counterfeit for everything. When we look at life through the world's perspective, these counterfeits seem to offer what we desire, but they only entice us in the wrong direction. A life separated from Him is a life in descent. But our inheritance is for the now. The revelation of Jesus Christ is His kingdom on earth, the same as it is in heaven—the answer has always been Jesus.

He created us to meet our trials, persecutions, and sicknesses with anticipation and expectancy for a revelation of His heart. The power of perseverance is an unprecedented reality of who we are in Christ. Anything that seems to be a reality in the moment can become a greater revelation of truth into eternity when illuminated by the Holy Spirit. These revelations are insights into the divine nature of who He is. This is the awakening of our spirit; it is destiny becoming our own reality while here on earth. Again, this is His kingdom, coming on earth as it is in heaven. No virtual reality is needed when our hearts are awakened to His divine reality and we are seeking out the treasure, the gold, of our blessed inheritance. And that is what He calls us to do.

CHAPTER TWELVE

The Quiet Place

*Be silent and stop your striving
and you will see that I am God.*
Psalm 46:10 tpt

It was the middle of the night, and suddenly, I was wide awake. I could identify no reason, no noise or movement that had awakened me, so eventually I went back to sleep. But then, it happened again the next night. And the next. And the next. I began getting up and going to the living room—sometimes to read, sometimes to pray, and sometimes just to sit in silence.

It's kind of silly when I think about it, how long it took me to consider that maybe the Holy Spirit was waking me up. I wasn't always comfortable in those quiet midnight moments. I'll admit that I even felt fearful of the silence at times. But as I recognized the wakefulness for what it was—God calling me to time with Him—I began looking forward to those quiet times together.

The magnitude of His peace, uninterrupted by the chaos of the world, has been so loud and the atmosphere at times so heavy that I have almost run for cover, but His perfect love is teaching me that I am created to be in His presence. His perfect love does indeed cast out all fear. I continue to be drawn into this quiet place of experiencing a profound invitation to enter deeper into His heart. It's a lovely place that I am certain He has reserved only for me.

This is what His divine peace does inside those who believe. He loves us so very intimately that we feel complete, yet at the same time, we grow lovesick, longing for the next quiet time we can be alone with our Creator—the One who loved us first and the One whose lovingkindness continues to draw us close.

The Holy Spirit is our resource for revelation of who Jesus is. Through Him, we receive the fullness of what God has for us. Our human bodies could never bear the weight of all His glory, but our spirits can receive the eternal depths of God's heart—we were created for such. Our outside tent will one day wither away, but our spirit will continue in His steadfast, exuberant love forever and ever, leaving time behind us.

God longs for His people to know Him. It is the sole purpose for Christ's sacrifice, for His death on that cross—so we could know Him. "Be still," He says, "and know that I am God"

(Psalm 46:10 NIV).

We can invite His silent stillness into our lives. He tells us how: "When you pray, go into your inner room, close your door, and pray to your Father who is in secret, and your Father who sees what is done in secret will reward you" (Matthew 6:6). When we spend time with Him, the physical world that revolves around time collides with eternity. The world comes to a pause because time, as we experience it, doesn't exist in His presence. And there in this moment, in this place, our physical senses receive a glimpse of eternity because perfect peace has entered our spirits and revealed Christ.

We experience these divine moments when our hearts and minds are fully turned toward Jesus. We must set aside every worldly responsibility and give Him our undistracted adoration and devotion. The silent stillness rushes in suddenly. The atmosphere changes, and the sense of awe we feel toward Jesus intensifies. These are heavenly moments; angels rejoice with us as we are still and know that He is God and that He is truly in this place.

In a chaotic and busy world, we treasure these moments, as we have both tasted and seen His goodness. With our senses acutely aware of Him and His presence, we become a people who live out the meaning of the Scripture, "I will fear no evil, for You are with me" (Psalm 23:4).

Revelation 8:1 speaks of heaven going silent for about half an hour in the presence of the Lamb. All creation falls silent with awe when His peace becomes our reality. There is so much power in this silence because the peace that *is* God resides there.

When we experience this peace, our eyes are opened, and our hearts receive the true revelation of Jesus Christ. We look at each person with new hope in the calling of our Lord. We see new value in each person. We see them through redemption's perspective. The highest price was paid for them.

When we choose to dwell on the One who is worthy of praise, our inner man becomes a place of continued revelation through the Holy Spirit. That continual revelation of Jesus enables us to see all creation through a new lens of purity and holiness. As we fix our gaze on Him, the things of this world that once consumed our thoughts become but a vapor.

Consider these great words from Philippians 4:8–9: "Finally, brethren, whatever is true, whatever is honorable, whatever is right, whatever is pure, whatever is lovely, whatever is of good repute, if there is any excellence and if anything is worthy of praise, dwell on these things . . . and the God of peace will be with you."

Matthew 13:44 tells us that "the kingdom of heaven is like a treasure hidden in the field, which a man found and hid again; and from joy over it he goes and sells all that he has and buys that field." Jesus is our treasure, and as we find Him and revelation begins, all the things that were fillers in our hearts become obsolete. We become a lovesick people with burning passion to know only His heart for more. Jesus Himself becomes our source of abundant life. His love overflows through us into the lives of those who we once held responsible for our happiness. Life flows outwardly from us when His life is revealed inwardly.

The real treasure, the gold we're digging for, is found in that secret place of our hearts. We hide our treasure (as mentioned in Matthew 13:44), but this is a good hiding. It's like we're wrapping our hearts around what we've found in this secret, private place. As we experience His joy, His overwhelming invitation asks us to come closer. We find ourselves selling the things of this world—our TV shows, social media accounts, and so on—they're all time wasted. We sell these things, and we buy the field where our treasure, our *gold*, is hidden. We buy the very kingdom of God with our hearts. That's all He has ever asked of us.

In exchange for our hearts, we inherit the kingdom of God. We find ourselves drawn to this secret place where we've hidden our treasure; we're drawn by His lovingkindness again and again. And in that place reserved only for Him, we are changed forever because we have been with the *Forever* of our hearts.

CHAPTER THIRTEEN

Quiet Listening

*The Helper, the Holy Spirit . . . will teach you all things,
and bring to your remembrance all that I said to you.*
John 14:26

There is no lie that has ever been told that can withstand the truth of His love when whispered by the Holy Spirit. Quiet times spent listening to Him in our secret places are the most magnificent of all. It's where the newness in us becomes even newer. Scripture promises that in that glorious place of abiding, nothing can separate us from His love: "For I am convinced that neither death, nor life, nor angels, nor principalities, nor things present, nor things to come, nor powers, nor height, nor depth, nor any created thing, will be able to separate us from the love of God, which is in Christ Jesus our Lord" (Romans 8:38–39).

Without intimate times of listening, however, we will continue in the conformity of the traditions of men and the ways of this world. Without the power of the Holy Spirit revealing Jesus to us, His Word cannot transform and renew us. That's why Romans 12:2 instructs that we should "not be conformed to this world, but be transformed by the renewing of your mind, so that you may prove what the will of God is, that which is good and acceptable and perfect." It's Him, always!

We witness transformation in people's lives as they are saved and changed by God's amazing grace. But too many times, new believers are encouraged to serve in the church, to join a small group, or to "get involved" more than they are encouraged to begin their intimate journey to relationship with Jesus. Unknowingly, we surround them with other believers whose initial transformation has ceased, and this almost always leads to disappointment.

At the beginning of our new life in Christ, His Spirit gives us new hope. He spiritually sets His joy in front of us, and we sense with excitement that our lives really can be different. This hope set before us is an invitation to partake of the new nature we have attained in knowing Him. But when these hopeful souls meet with believers who have not continued their own growth in knowing Jesus, they can be led astray. Sometimes they choose to head back out into the world, and sometimes they step into a life filled with religious hypocrisies.

We can avoid this. That newfound hope will flourish when we encourage each other toward Him, toward seeking that resting place in His heart. Living life in the Spirit is an unfamiliar experience for the new believer, so we must help them establish a firm foundation of intentionally spending time getting to know Jesus. This is why we should encourage each other to pull away from the chaos of the world and allow Jesus to become our cornerstone. This is how our first love *becomes* our first love. We fall in love because we yield to the unmistakable drawing of His lovingkindness (Jeremiah 31:3). We fall in love with love, and it's in this place of knowing Him that we will never stumble (2 Peter 1:10).

We all become ministers to Jesus during this time. He is our first ministry. When our lives are lived to love Him, every other "ministry" in our life will be nourished with the fruit of the Spirit that is produced from our first ministry. "But the fruit of the Spirit is love, joy, peace, patience, kindness, goodness, faithfulness, gentleness, self-control; against such things there is no law" (Galatians 5:22–23).

This is God's divine design. The better we know Him, the more we love Him, and that produces all that we'll ever need to become everything He intends us to be. A heart that is devoted to God becomes a heart that is addicted to God. We become His. Our hearts burn just to know Him more. We find our resting place in Him, and we never have to leave. We become a people who love Him with all our hearts, minds, and souls (Matthew 22:37).

Our Father is infinitely loving and patient. We pray for the things we think we desire, and in His lovingkindness, He gives us many of them. All the while, He patiently waits for us to choose first to seek His kingdom and His righteousness. *"Come closer,"* He whispers, as He draws us near.

The time we spend privately seeking Jesus is dangerous to the enemy who rules this world. Truth brings power, and power brings strength to change every old thing. As Satan notices a person seeking truth, he will rear his ugliness in more strategic ways. He'll bring distraction from every angle, but with diligence we can overcome each of them.

Our effort to overcome those obstacles of distraction gives the Holy Spirit what He desires—our attention and devotion. With these, He can set our hearts ablaze. With the Holy Spirit's revelation of the person of Jesus to us, His Word becomes alive in us. When we spend time with Him, He opens the door of truth to us that no man will talk us out of. His truth also removes the traditional mindsets that have been passed down to us from generation to generation. His heart's pleasure is to see us set free—and we will be free. Free indeed!

Being with Him this way creates a passion in our hearts for things of His spirit. Authentic relationship with Him initiates a desire in our hearts to see other lives changed. Love becomes our nature, and we become confident in His desire to draw every heart into His. This confidence comes from the secret place of experiencing Him in such a way that you know in the depths of your soul that the pure and holy amazing grace that has washed over you was poured out also for all humanity.

A heart that *remembers* His passion on the cross becomes a heart that *experiences* His passion on the cross. Hearing His words, "Father, forgive them; for they do not know what they are doing" (Luke 23:34) as a passionate cry to the Father births an unadulterated revelation of love. Any question of His desire that all would know Him is answered at the cross, and the passion of His resounding yes comes crashing into our hearts. We become passionate representatives of His gospel, unable to neglect this sacrifice, because hearing those words from the cross awakens our spirits. They penetrate our hearts and leave us longing to know Him even more. In this place, He becomes our hearts' song. He becomes our one desire!

CHAPTER FOURTEEN

Baptism

*And I remembered the word of the Lord, how He used to
say, "John baptized with water, but you will be baptized
with the Holy Spirit."*
Acts 2:38

There are many conversations over the baptism of the Holy
Spirit, but one thing is certain—Jesus, and He alone, is the
baptizer of the Holy Spirit and fire. Men baptize us with water.
Jesus baptizes us by immersing our beings into the Holy Spirit and
fire. This baptism looks different for every person. But regardless
of how it happens, His purpose of purifying our hearts will ac-
complish His will and allow us to continue the journey into even
holier places with Him. He is a multifaceted, multidimensional,
fascinating holy purifier who enters in with fire and powerfully dis-
integrates every impurity that has taken up residence in our souls.
This is the process of the journey for a heart that follows His. The
windows of our souls are cleansed, and our eyes are opened wide.

This holy baptism is a continual filling of Him for those of us
in this glorious relationship. When we have a continuous desire
to know Him, that is when His fire is free to purify—because we
choose to stir that flame the Holy Spirit fueled in us, the flame that
will never go out. He gives us His heart; He lavishes us with His
love. We give our hearts back in return, loving Him, trusting Him
with a life of unending praise.

He purifies us for one purpose—to draw us closer to Him.

The purification by fire and the weight of His righteousness invade the old man in us and nothing old can remain. The experience of receiving the fire looks different for each of us because, just as we are individually and wonderfully created by Him, so is His purpose for each of us unique.

The baptism of the Holy Spirit has been an ongoing event in my journey of wholeheartedly seeking the Lord. With my whole heart, I believe that He fills me daily as I come to Him to be cleansed by His purifying fire. He never purifies or empties those places in me without filling me with Himself, with His streams of living water. This infilling of the Holy Spirit, this process of liquid love, so to speak, has been part of my sanctification process.

We each have our own testimony of our personal experience of His baptism. These beautifully different testimonies are witness to His diverse purposes for each of us and His immense intentionality of intimate relationship in every life that seeks to know Him.

I would even say the baptism for us is the same as nurturing parents who wash their children daily in a bath—it's a wonderful act of love for the parents to wash away the dirt from the world. And in the same way Jesus in this relationship, the baptism continues daily as He cleanses us of the exposures of the evil days in the world. It's funny to think that sometimes babies and children go through periods of time when they fuss about taking a bath. It can be a battle even, and parents teach them about obedience as they insist that bathing is an important part of our lives. As children grow and experience the feeling of being clean, they grow into enjoying the feeling of being refreshed that bathing brings—and before you know it, they are their own person desiring to wash away the dirt from the day.

In our relationship with Jesus, many things begin in obedience, and the outcome of obedience will always bring us to a place of being cleansed, as Jesus continues the baptism. The beautiful thing about this relationship is that as He cleanses us again and again, we experience His love again and again. Our obedience early on as baby Christians will mature us to a place that our hearts long for and desire, to this ongoing baptism of the Holy Spirit. Because every cleansing by the Holy Spirit will then lead us into refreshing moments of God's true character being revealed to us.

CHAPTER FIFTEEN

Treasure Chest

The disciple that Jesus dearly loved was . . .
leaning his head on Jesus.
John 13:23 TPT

As John rested on the chest of Jesus, he could physically hear and know that Jesus loved him. He was in a beautiful place with Jesus—he could clearly hear the heartbeat of our Lord saying: *come closer and be still.*

I had a vision once of a beautiful treasure chest. The dream was alive and heavenly, brilliant, diamond-like glitter sparkled in the electrified atmosphere. The chest itself was wrapped in a beautiful red bow.

The bow is the gift of the blood of Jesus—His invitation to enter in. Those seeking Him will find the key that unlocks the treasure of all treasures—the secret places of His heart. Now, just as John was resting on Jesus's chest (John 13:22), Jesus is our way to rest on God's chest—the place where every treasure is hidden.

God created us for Himself. He created us to live inside His heart—His treasure *chest*! He has prepared this place for us and waits there to reveal the treasures of life. The more we dig inside this place, the more He reveals Himself to us.

In the beginning, God created us with a heart of flesh, a heart that was created to beat at the same steady rate as His. Adam could hear the beat of God's heart coming toward him as He walked in the garden. That heart was pumping a steady flow of living water, pure and holy—the very blood that was shed on the cross for us. We were created to have that same blood pumping through our veins. But Adam's sinful choice separated us from that heart.

God did not leave us to perish, however. He had a plan. He would sacrifice all of who He was to become sin, the very sin Adam and Eve chose that day in the garden. That dreadful day on the cross, the purity of God was emptied out of Jesus's body. All the treasures of life in His Spirit were separated from the eternal source of life everlasting. As He sacrificed His life source and His body was emptied of His blood, He became sin. He experienced death.

As Jesus hung on that cross, He cried out, saying, "My God, My God, why have You forsaken Me?" (Matthew 27:46). In those moments, He experienced the horrific separation that sin causes us to experience. Distance from a Father who has promised to never leave us, separation from the Creator of all things, who holds all things together. The One who is the same today as He was and has always been. Jesus, as the son of man, experienced for us what the lies and deception of the enemy would inflict upon us. Jesus, as the son of man, experienced what seemed like the abandonment of God.

We must understand that, in any situation or circumstance where we think God has abandoned us or is not speaking to us, we are being deceived. Our great God promised to never leave us, yet even Jesus felt abandoned. I tell you, however, God was there. Sin stood between them, but He never left. For Jesus, just as it is for us, those feelings of distance and separation were the result of sin. Sin comes through listening to anything other than the words of our loving Father.

Jesus walked this earth to show us what it would look like to have a heart of flesh and a spirit unified with God. He lived the life we were created to live. This was God's original dream, His divine design—a people choosing Him and loving Him with hearts

He'd created to thrive along with Him, their veins flooded with the source of life—God's living water.

With that living water absent from His body, Jesus descended into hell. He chose to experience death—that separation from God we were never intended to know—so we wouldn't have to. This separation is a pit of descension without an end, and it is the horrific reality that those who choose not to believe in Jesus will ultimately face.

By Adam and Eve's choice, the knowledge of the tree of good and evil was exposed to all mankind. It was the defining moment of separation. It was the moment that our hearts turned from flesh to stone. Man chose to turn away from God's divine design, but in His infinite love, Jesus chose to sacrifice His life blood, His own heart of flesh, to bring us back. His sacrifice gives us the chance to come back home, to choose the divine life source of living water.

From the very beginning, our choices have defined our destinies. Lean close to the heart of Jesus. Step into the throne room. Dig deep into the treasure chest of His infinite love.

CHAPTER SIXTEEN

Freedom and Victory

Do not worry about tomorrow,
for tomorrow will care for itself.
Matthew 6:34

How different would our lives look if we chose to live in freedom and victory? What if we believed that the message of the cross includes a life of victory for the here and now?

Through His death and resurrection, Jesus overcame Satan, the ruler of this world, and in His victory, He has transferred to us His full authority (Luke 10:19). We claim that power and authority when we choose to believe Him, to believe that He overcame the ruler of this world so His children could live in freedom from all fear.

Too often, our actions reflect those of people who fear flesh, but God says our war is not against flesh. We lock our doors and protect our homes with the best security systems. We carry weapons and live in gated communities. We watch the news to be aware of the latest ugly story. We buy insurance against every possibility—if we fear something could happen to it, we insure it: our jewelry, cars, pets, houses, health, even our lives. After all, we've so much to prepare for: education, vacation, retirement, the list goes on. We've become a society living in fear. We don't know what tomorrow holds, so we prepare in every way imaginable.

But Jesus told us to live differently. "Do not worry about tomorrow," He said, "for tomorrow will care for itself. Each day has enough trouble of its own" (Matthew 6:34). Fear causes distraction that can flood our lives with false concerns for tomorrow. It can steal away today's opportunity for abundant life. All the decisions we make, focused on preparing for tomorrow, cause us to reek of anxiety. But anxiety from the world's concerns gives fear a place to roost in our lives—a place where only freedom should reside.

People claim these concerns are logical. They say that since God gave us brains, we should use them to ensure our safety for the future. But He gave us our brains so we could choose faith over fear. We must stop the chaos that fear causes. Fear separates us from God's glorious promise—from the future He holds and the abundant life He offers.

When we focus on Him instead of fear, every decision we make is from a place of hope in Him. In faith, we invite Him to be our God so all the world can see His magnificent love and provision. Do we believe that all our hope is found in Him? If we do, we can take these worries of the world and literally, in our spirits, give them to the Father. First Peter 5:7 speaks directly to each believer: "Cast all your anxiety on him, because he cares for you" (NIV).

There have been concerns in my life that I have had to deliberately hand over to God. Free of the worry over those problems, I've chosen to settle into living with thanksgiving and praise, to camp out in His courts. I've found that my faith grows and my spiritual territory expands when I choose to trust Him in those uncertain places. There, my knowledge of Him as my magnificent Father who cares for me increases. I have had to offer a sacrifice of praise many times over real worldly concerns.

We are surrounded by many who live in that place of fear, but we as His believers and children must learn to trust Him. Our decisions reflect what we believe. Where we put our trust determines who we spend time listening to. Our lives will sparkle with His radiant truth and a beautiful hope for the future when our decisions reflect that we believe the gospel.

These are defining moments in our lives. The choices we make in the natural reflect who we trust in the spirit. Every time we choose to believe that our war is not with the flesh of men, we grow in our faith. It's an amazing way to live, choosing to believe that God is involved in every detail of our lives. And He is—He's right there waiting for us to become aware of His goodness. Let us take seriously our one command to love Him with all our hearts, all our minds, and all our souls.

True freedom and victory are found in loving Him with every fiber of who we are. When we surrender our lives to Him, we are free from the anxieties of the world. We are free to know Him more, to be so intimately acquainted with Him that we trust Him implicitly all along the way.

CHAPTER SEVENTEEN

Pure and Holy

Whatever is true, whatever is noble, whatever is pure,
whatever is lovely, whatever is admirable—if anything
is excellent or praiseworthy—think about such things.
Philippians 4:8 NIV

Purity and holiness are misunderstood by society and completely misrepresented by religion. Religion portrays purity and holiness as unattainable because even the laws we're taught to follow are unable to fulfill all that purity and holiness require. Society peers through religion's stained-glass windows and sees only a people who, at best, are struggling to help each other deal with the stains of the past. Not understanding then, society mocks those who are overwhelmed by the realities of sin and shortcomings.

Many times, those who are falling short are people who have been touched by God's amazing grace. The knowledge of their shortcoming is how their hearts were enlightened to their need of a Savior, but they are stuck at the place of knowing they need Him. They believe that salvation's only purpose is to forgive their sins against a pure and holy God. They do not understand the full potential of what God offers.

These people hear talk of being pure and holy, and they know they aren't. They feel far from God because they still carry the stains of their past. That knowledge should not discourage them, however. It should be the beginning of a desire to better know the One who died for them. Instead, they get caught in the words of 1 Peter 1:16, where God said, "Be holy, for I am holy."

Religion does not teach an understanding of purity and holiness. Instead, it teaches that the characteristics of God are unattainable, untouchable, and far from us. The stained-glass windows of our religious hindering portray the holiness of God as something reserved for our eyes to see only through the lens of our guilt. It is a view of what He is and what we are not.

We forget that His grace is provided to cover and rescue us from our past and daily sinful natures, and we get stuck. We become an unholy people whose idea of purity is skewed by our sin-stained eyes. We're a people in waiting, wishing for our Savior to come and take us out of this sinful world that we think we are powerless against.

But I want to tell you something. *Jesus would not tell us to be holy if holiness was not possible!* Everything that He says for us in His Word that we think is impossible becomes reality when we turn our hearts toward knowing Him and trusting Him more. His desire is that we would be so close to Him that we could experience the true revelation of Him through the Holy Spirit. Then our lives would be new and purified.

God is looking for a holy people, walking in the purity of who they have become in His loving presence. Being holy and pure becomes our reality only as He becomes our dwelling place. Pure and holy—these are attributes much different than we have thought. They are reachable, touchable, and livable. They are treasures we will find when we choose to dig for the gold that is hidden in His heart. As we search for His treasure, purity and holiness become attributes of who we are—because of what He has done.

The purest thing, the holiest thing, the most inexpressible thing is Jesus. His love is His person. His love is His nature. His nature is love. His character is love. *God is love.*

Every expression of love, throughout all of time, originated in who He is. Love has an original source—God Himself. Love was not just an idea God had and decided to express from time to time by telling us stories of love throughout His Word. No. The expression of His love is seen inside each mystery, and these mysteries invite us to search for ourselves inside the heart of God. We become explorers, treasure hunters, *gold diggers*, who find the deepest treasures as His love unfolds. We find our destiny as we live every day inside the fullness of God.

He created us for His heart's pleasure. Inside the treasure box of His heart are all His promises, fulfilled and waiting to be revealed. He just wants relationship with us, not religion! Digging for this gold is not striving or working hard to study every theory or historical bit of evidence. These invitations are of the heart; they are found in rest. The Holy Spirit reveals His mysteries, and revelatory moments flow through our beings as we give Him freedom and room to roam in our souls. And He fills every space with truth.

As we grow in relationship, we begin to look for our bridegroom, Jesus. We love Him with all our hearts, minds, and souls. And when we are gold diggers *of* our King Jesus, we become qualified as gold diggers *for* King Jesus. That's when we can fulfill the second and only other command He gave us.

We can love our neighbor as we love ourselves because we have truly experienced the love of God. We can now dig for gold in every person the world has thrown away.

We are the gold diggers—we can reveal the mysteries of God's by digging the gold out of every other person's heart. The mysterious and passionate love demonstrated on the cross is lived out by those who are filled with His holy fire. Spiritual warfare is won when we love from this authentic place, because love is the place where Satan is overcome.

We become the church of Christ when the revelation of Christ is our banner. We can proclaim the revelation that the cross is not a burden to carry as a reminder of all we've done wrong. No, it is our passionate evidence of all He has done so we could know God, the lover of our souls.

Now to Him who is able to keep you from stumbling,
and to make you stand in the presence of His glory blameless
with great joy,
to the only God our Savior, through Jesus Christ our Lord, be
glory, majesty, dominion,
and authority, before all time and now and forever. Amen.
Jude 1:24–25

Order Information

To order additional copies of this book, please visit
www.redemption-press.com.
Also available on Amazon.com and BarnesandNoble.com
or by calling toll-free 1-844-2REDEEM.

CPSIA information can be obtained
at www.ICGtesting.com
Printed in the USA
LVHW091124110221
678886LV00008B/635